RAISED BY OUR FATHER

Tshreletso and Boitumelo

Dedication

Esther – our dear beloved mother. We truely miss you.

Table of Contents

Boitumelo:

GRANNY HOUSE – Granny gets inside the house so she can watch television.

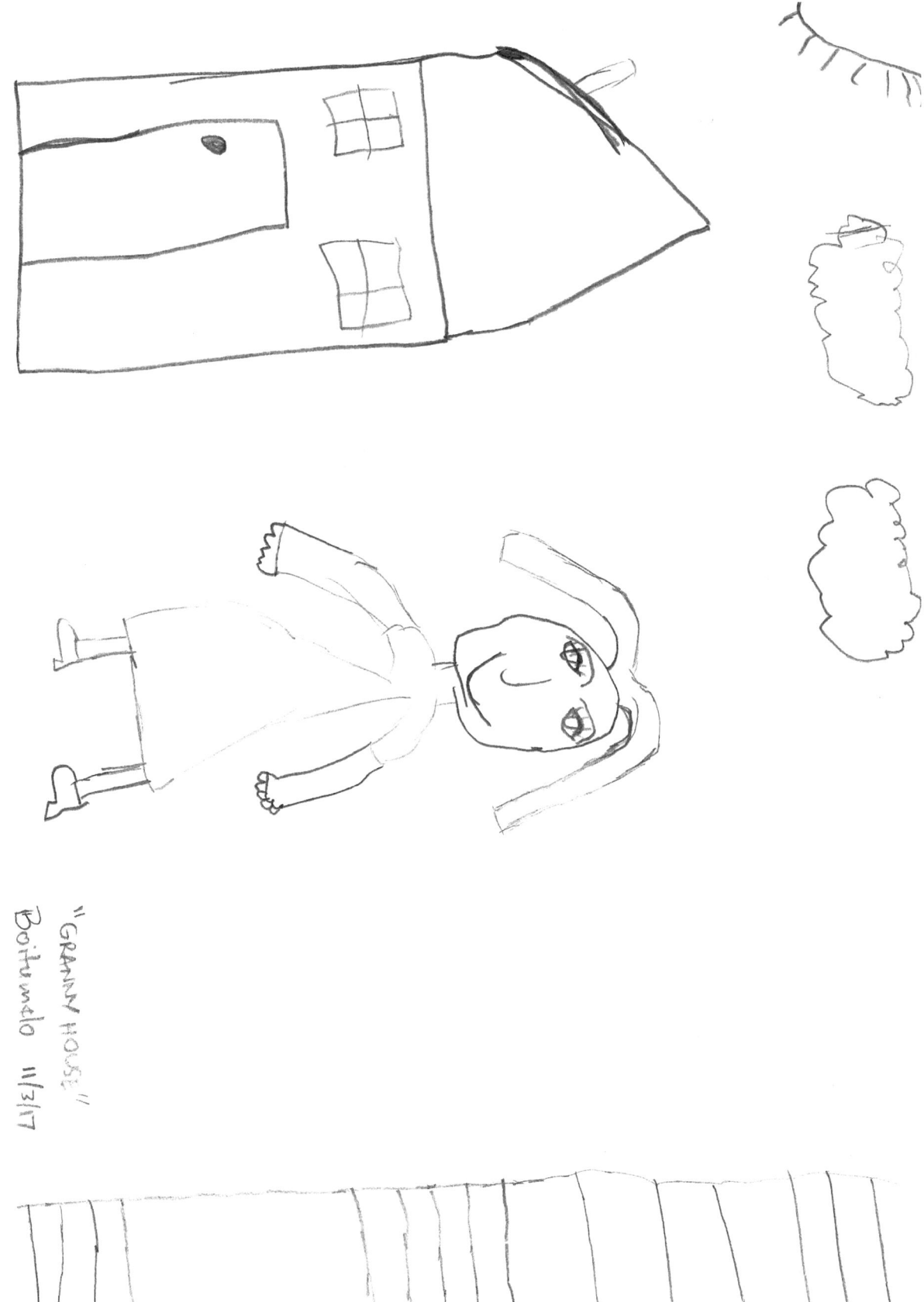

"GRANNY HOUSE"
Boitumelo 11/3/17

6

GRANNY WATCHING TELEVISION – Granny watches the news on the television in her living room in Alex.

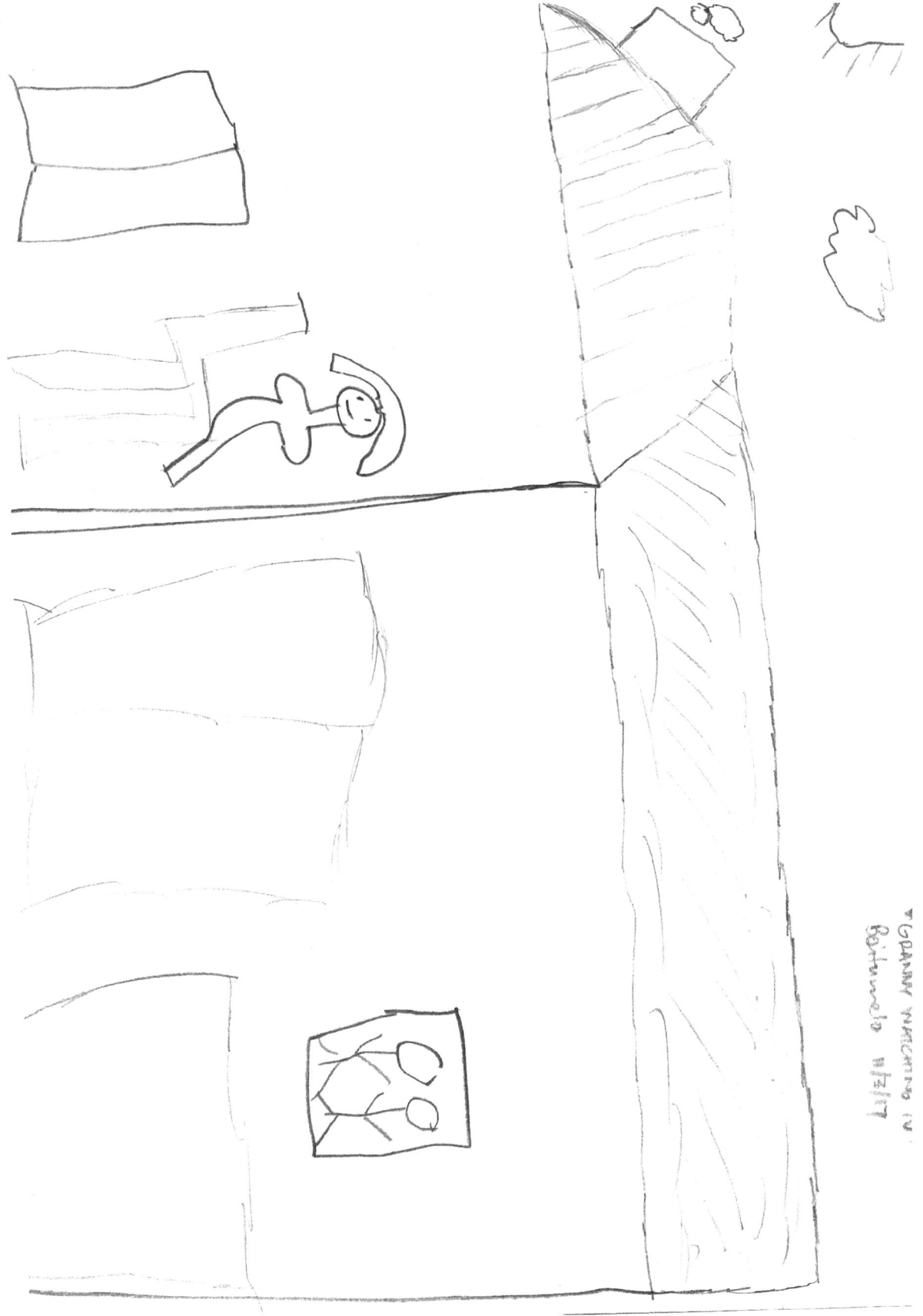

"GRANNY WATCHING TV"
Rothwell's NILEY

8

MOTHER SLEEPING – Mother is tired, she sleeps on the bed in her bedroom.

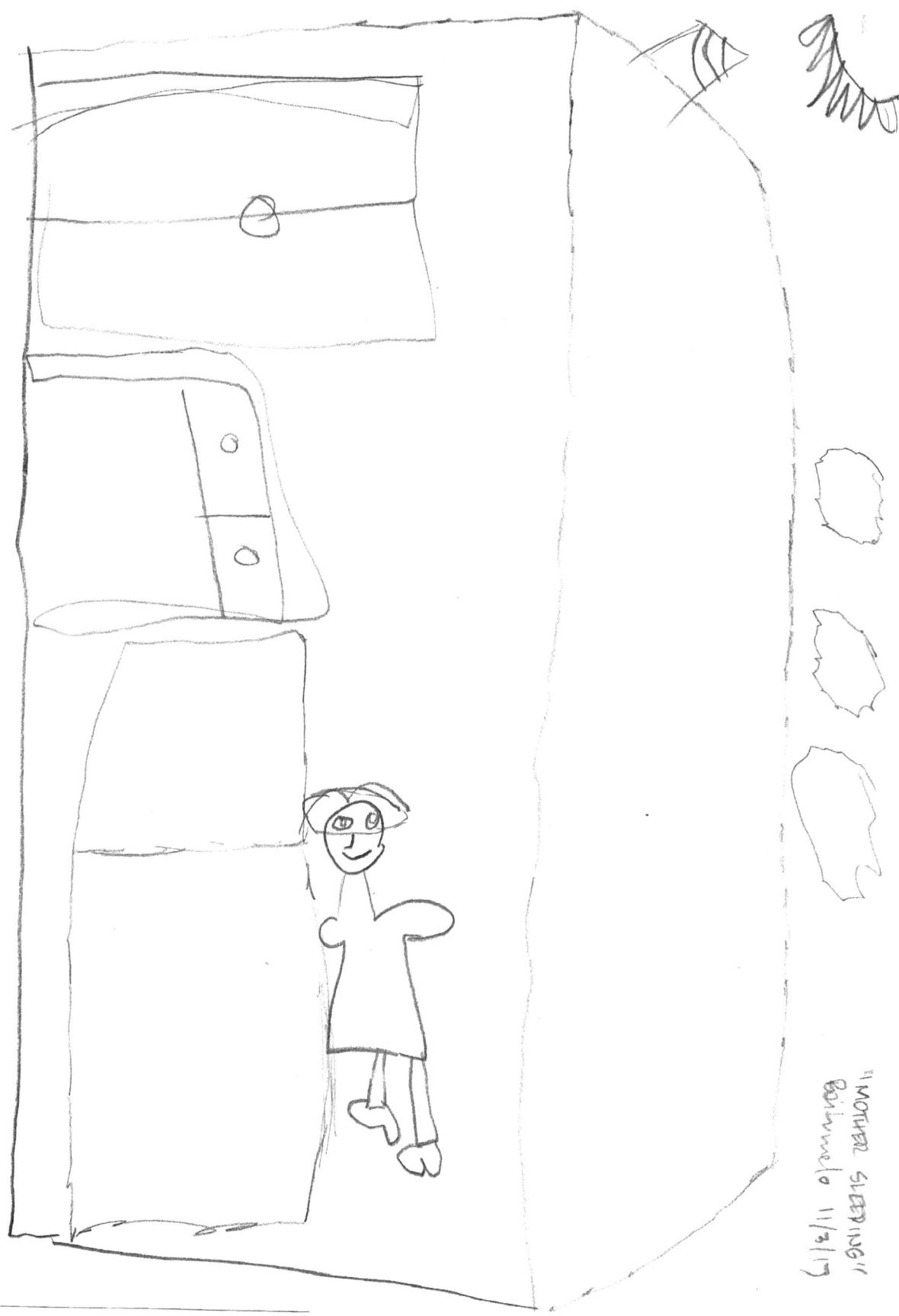

"MOTHER SLEEPING"
Emanuelo 11/3/11
6/3/11

FAMILY – My family in a restaurant.

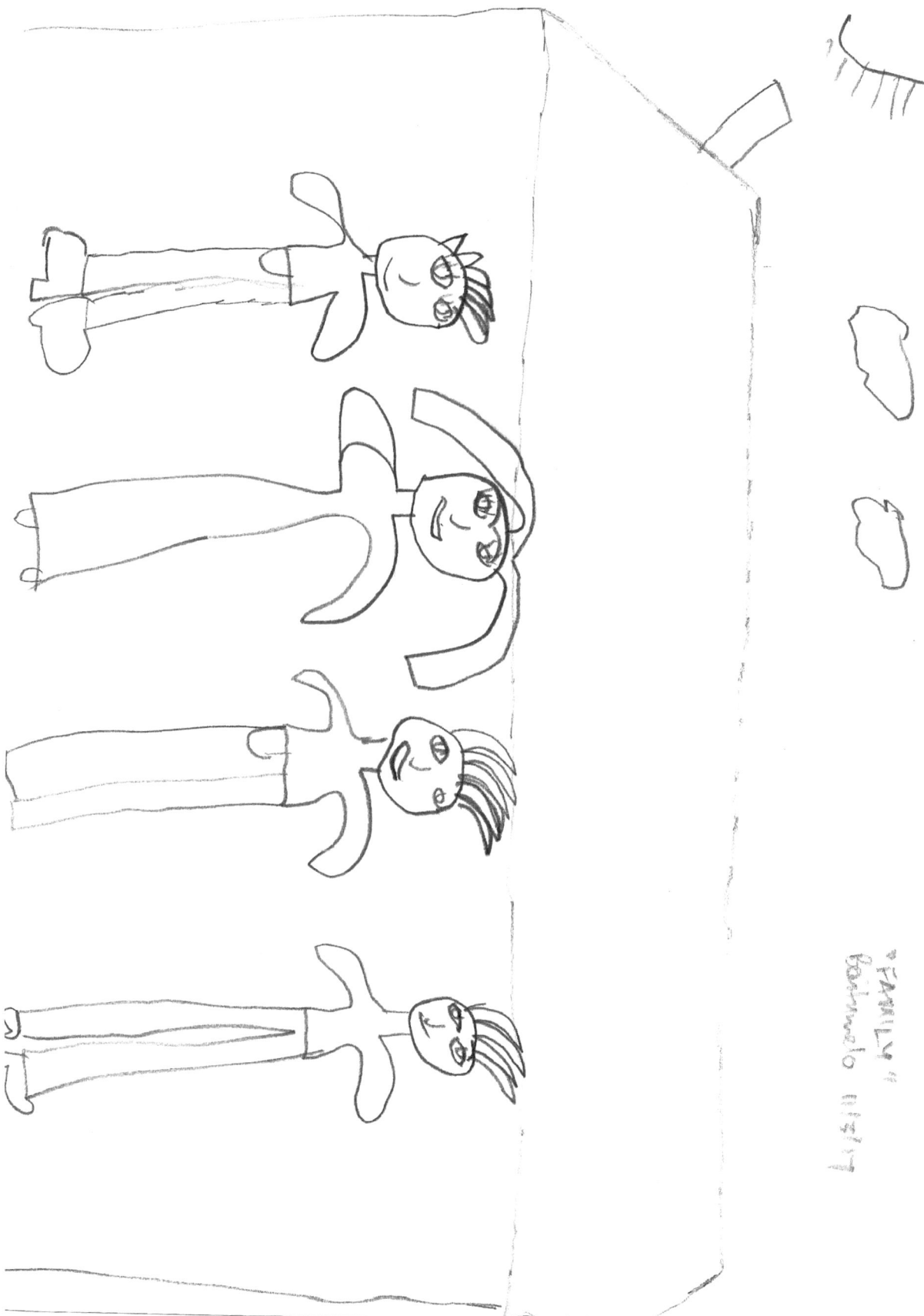

PULL-UP PLACE- My friend doing pull-ups in a gym park near our house in Edenvale.

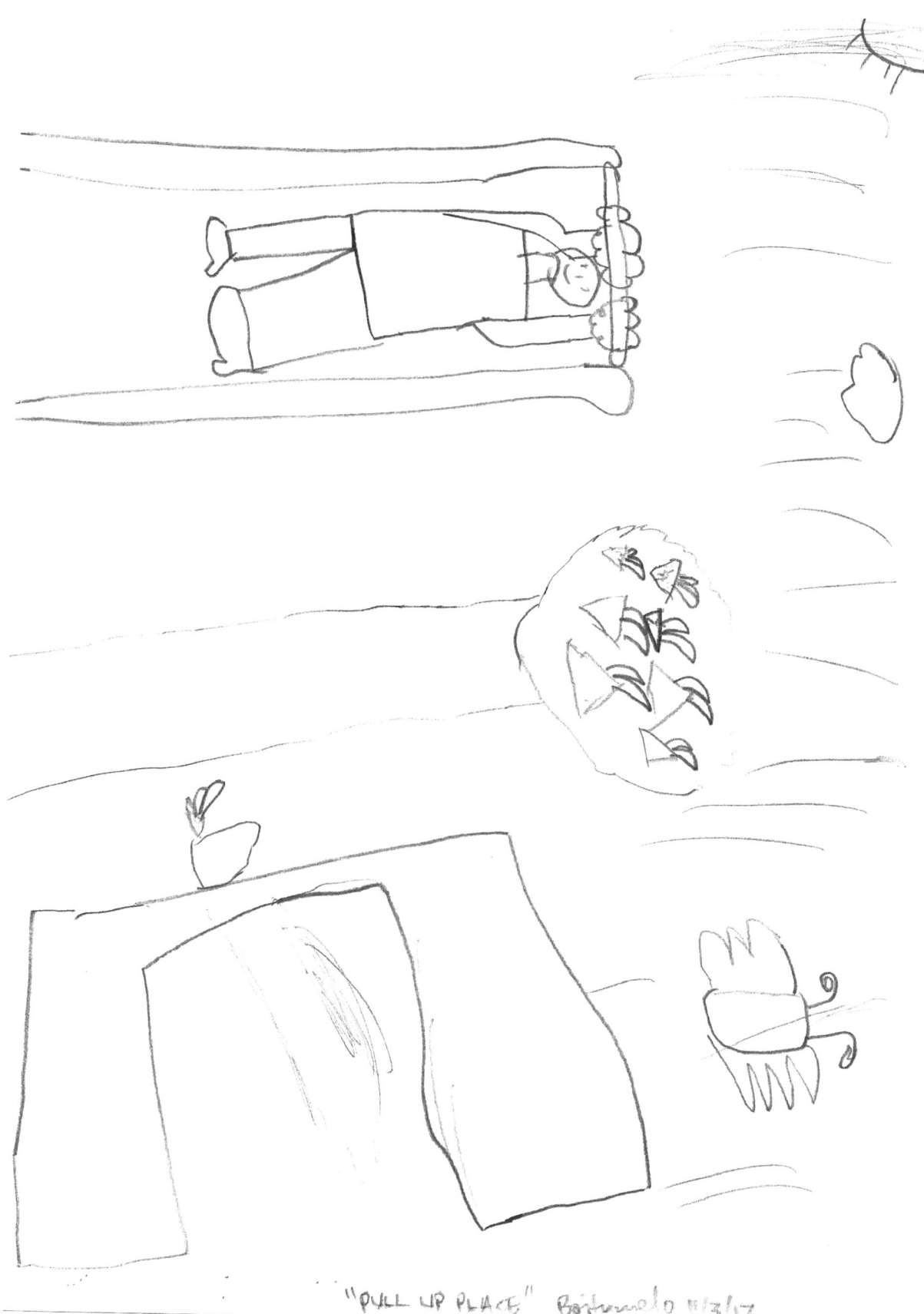

"PULL UP PLACE" Bartimelo 11/3/17

MAMLAMBO – River Queen makes rain and thunder.

"MAMLAMBO"
Bérthmelo 11/3/17

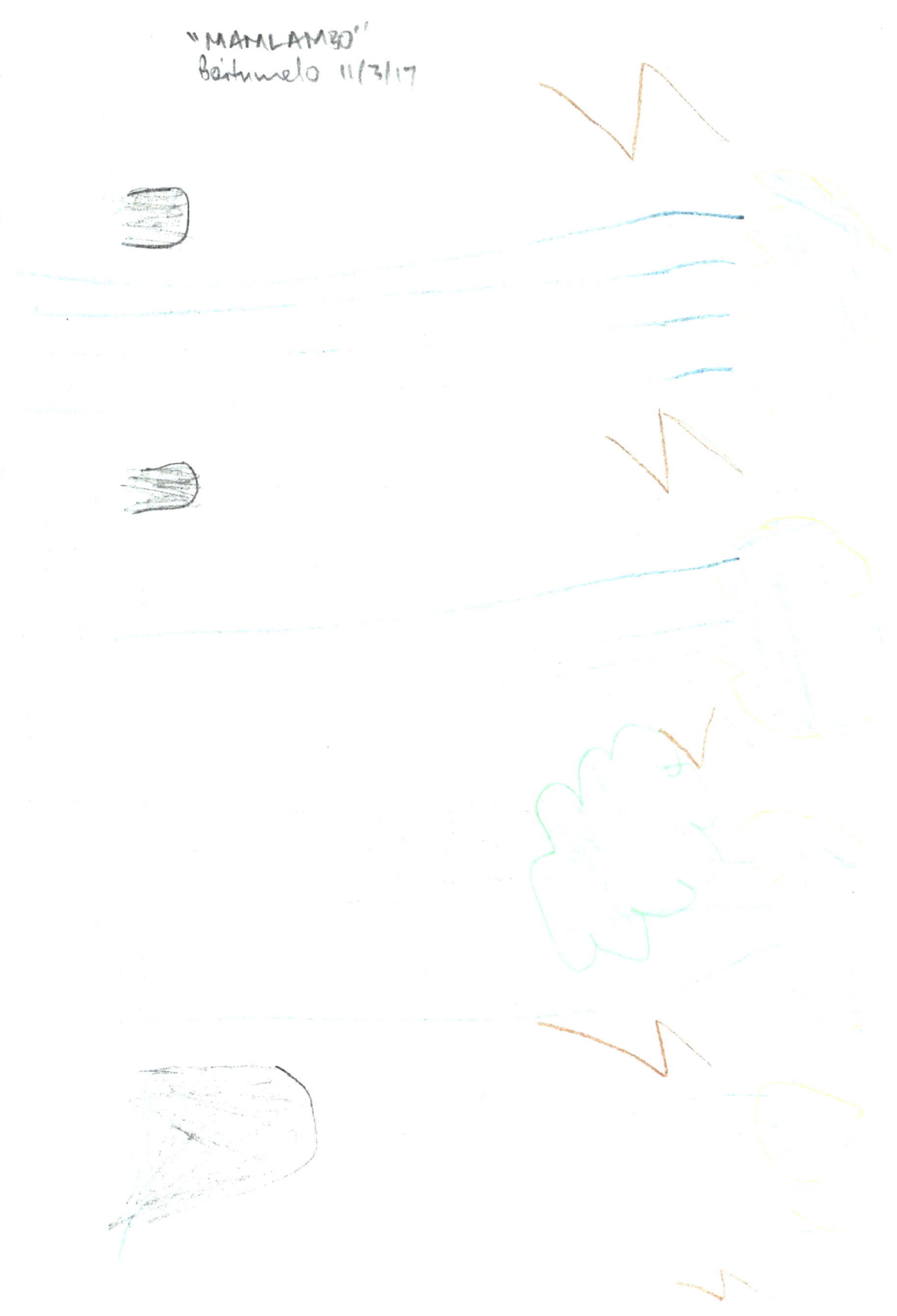

CLASSROOM – I am asking my Teacher to go to the toilet (bathroom).

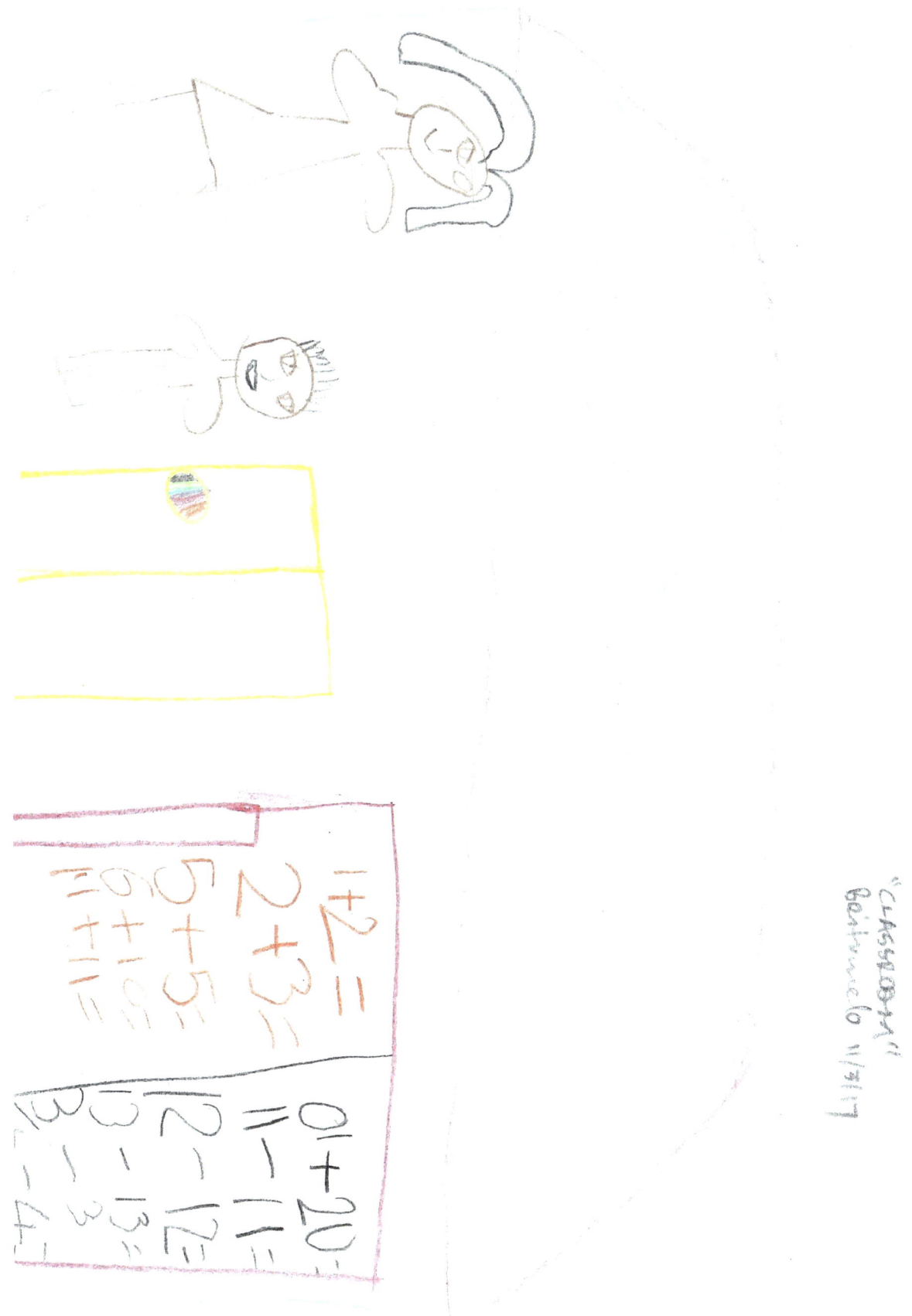

1+2=
2+3=
5+5=
6+10=
1+1=

10+20=
1-1=
2-1=
13-3=
13-4=

"CLASSROOM"
Beatrice 6 11/7

18

GRANNY AND MOM – My mother and grandmother, getting inside the house in Alexandria.

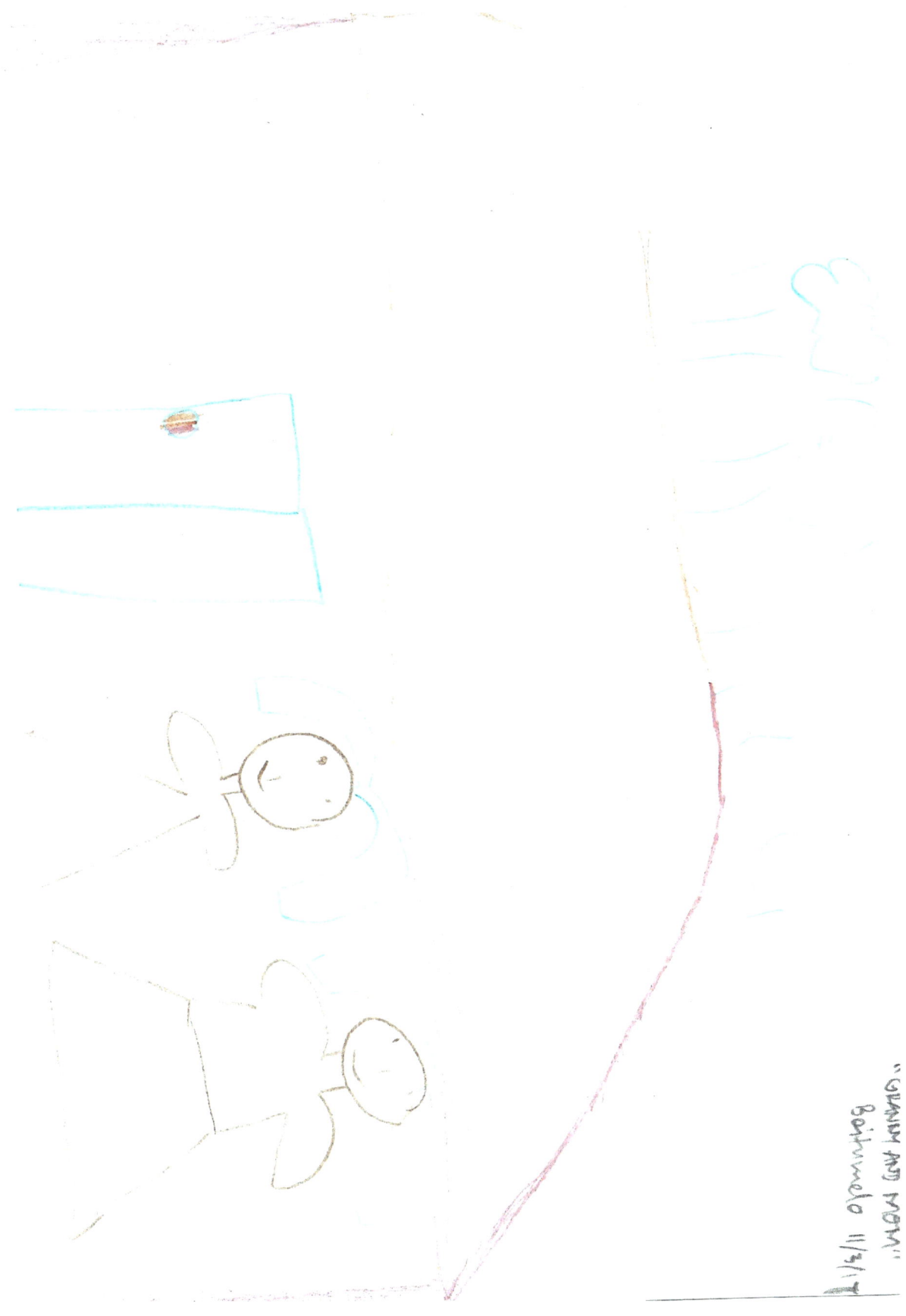

"GRANNY AND MOM"
Boitumelo 11/3/11

BEACH – AT THE BEACH IN DURBAN, SWIMMING WITH OUR MOTHER – ME AND MY BROTHER.

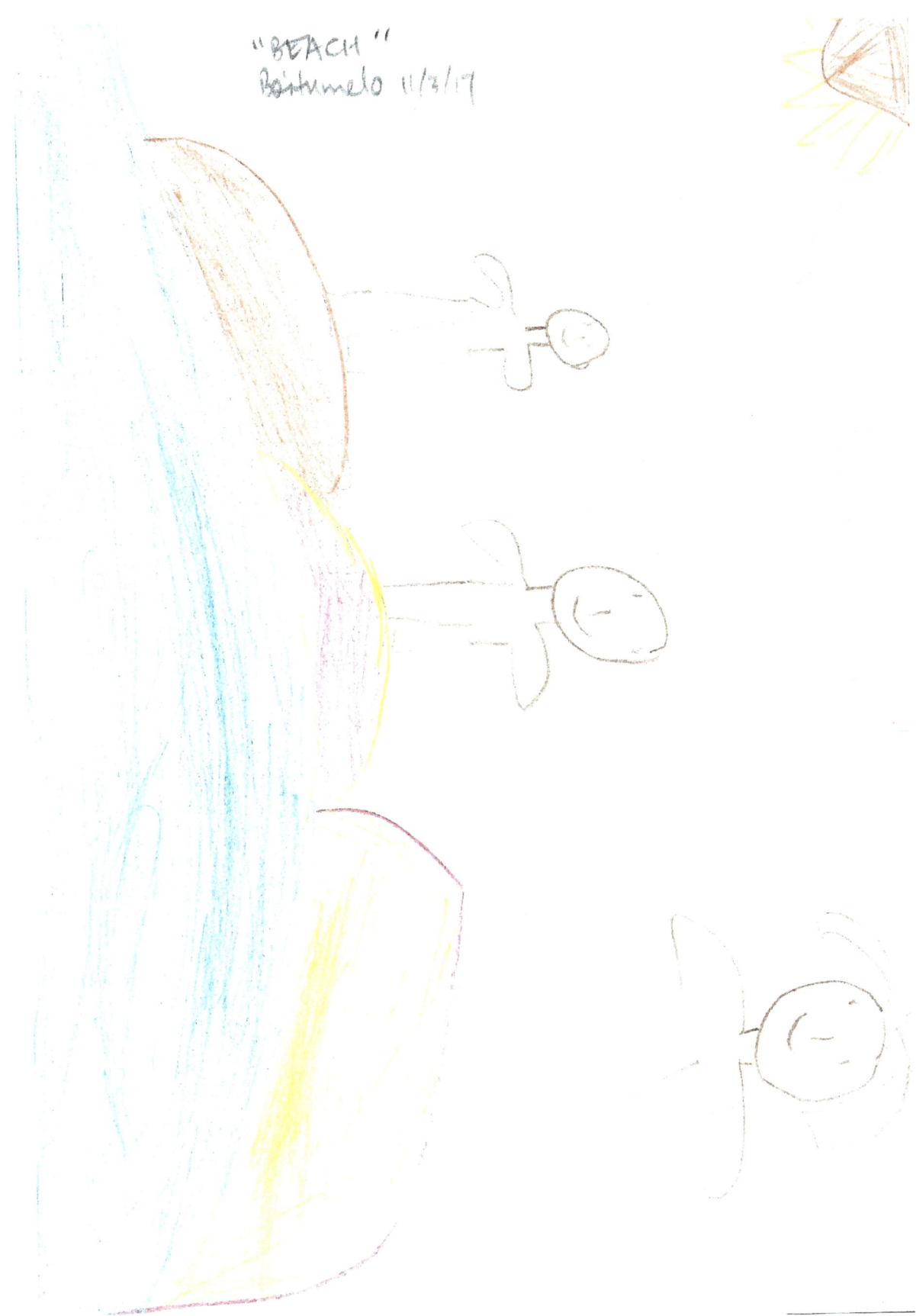

"BEACH"
Boitumelo 11/3/17

SOCCER MATCH – Playing a soccer match with my best friend, and people are watching.

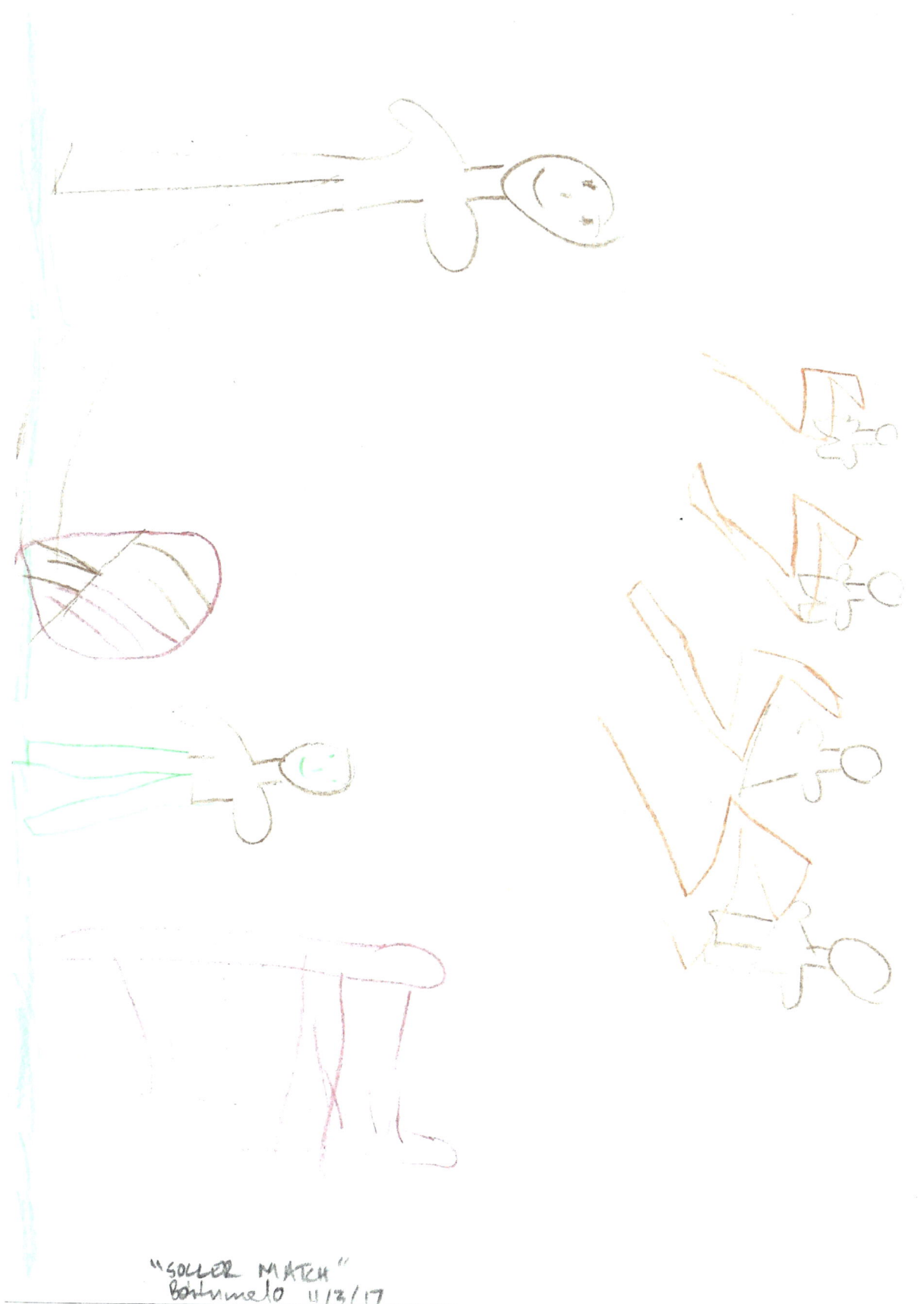

"SOCCER MATCH"
Bartumelo 11/3/17

Tshreletso:

HOUSE IN ALEX – The car is parked in our yard on 2nd Avenue, Alexandria.

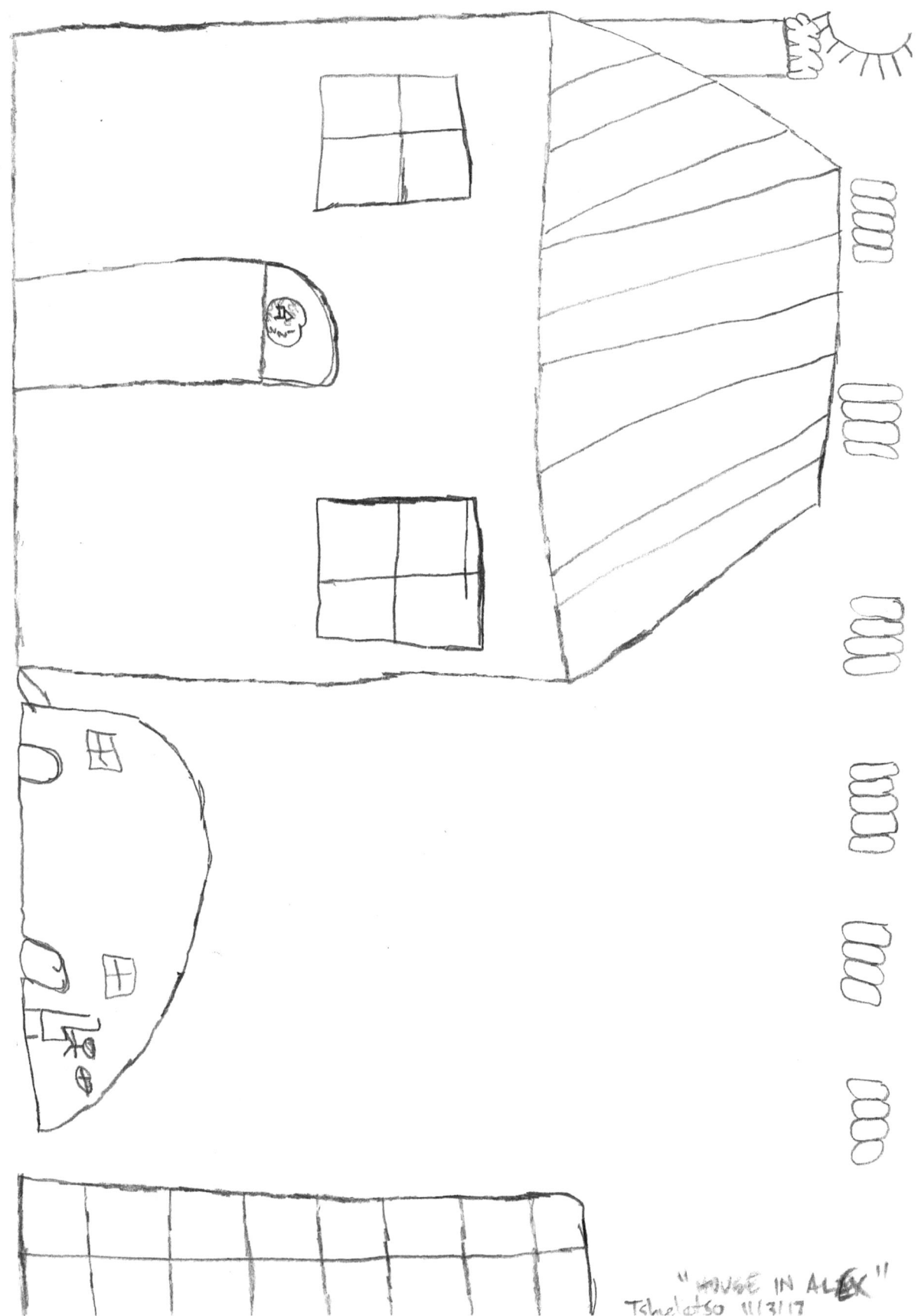

"HOUSE IN ALEX"
Tshelatso 11/3/17

GRANNY WATCHING TV – My granny is watching television while we make food for her.

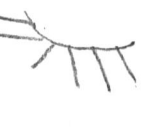

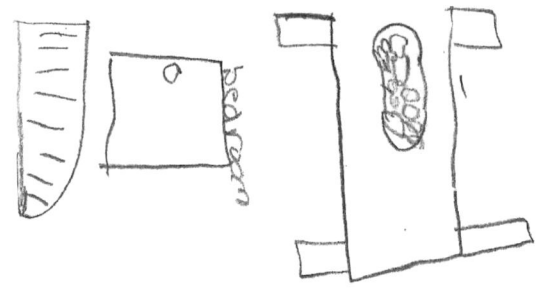

bedroom

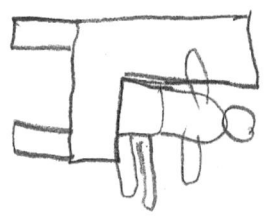

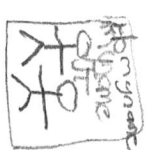

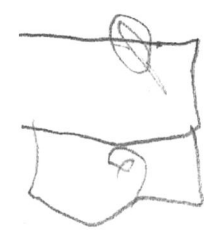

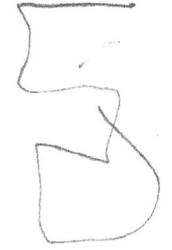

"GRANDMA WATCHING TV"
TSWU OSO 11/7/17

MY FAMILY – Eating pizza and drinking milkshake with my family.

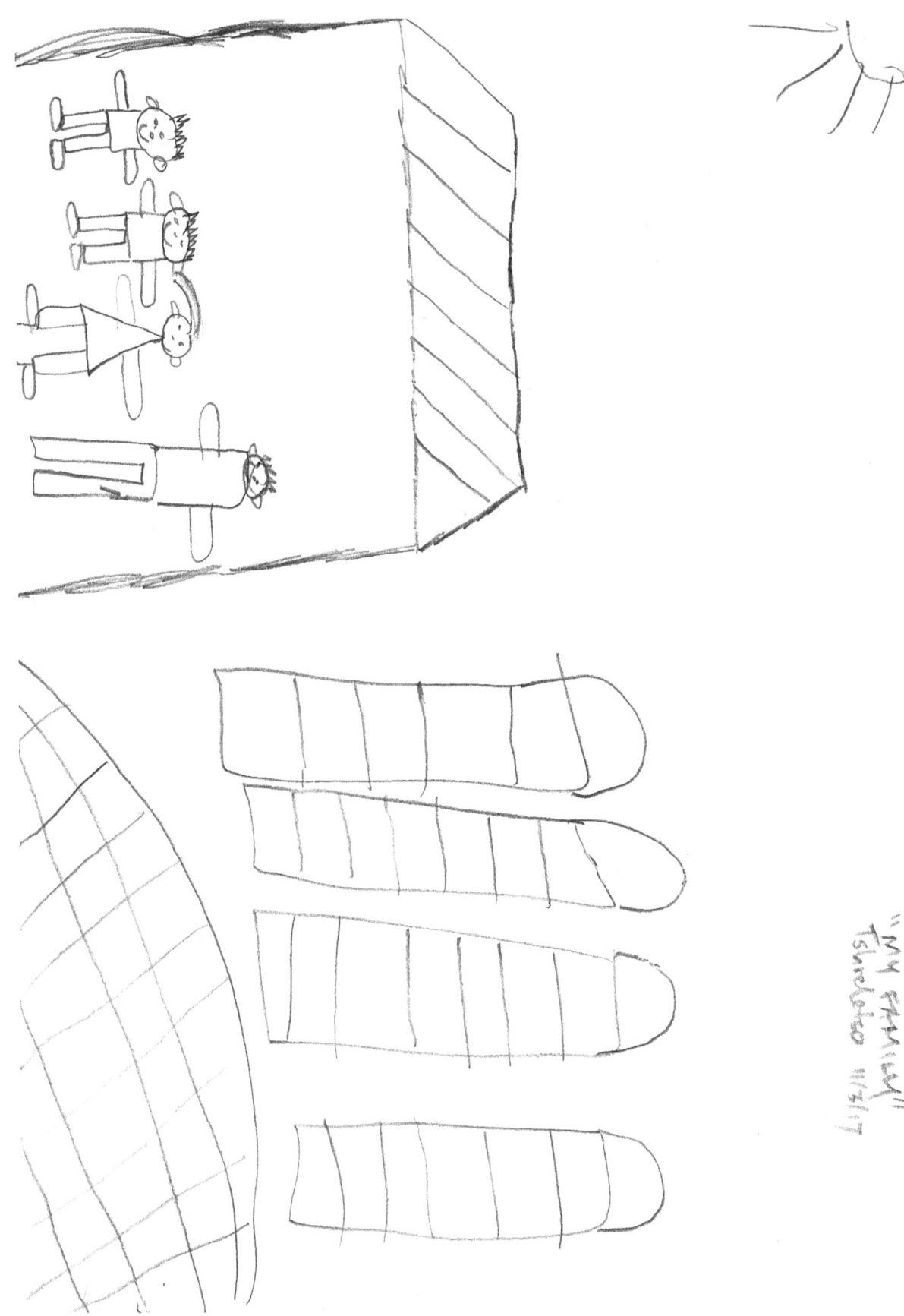

"MY FAMILY"
Tsireledzo 11/3/17

FAMILY OUTING – Playing soccer in the park with my family and it starts to rain.

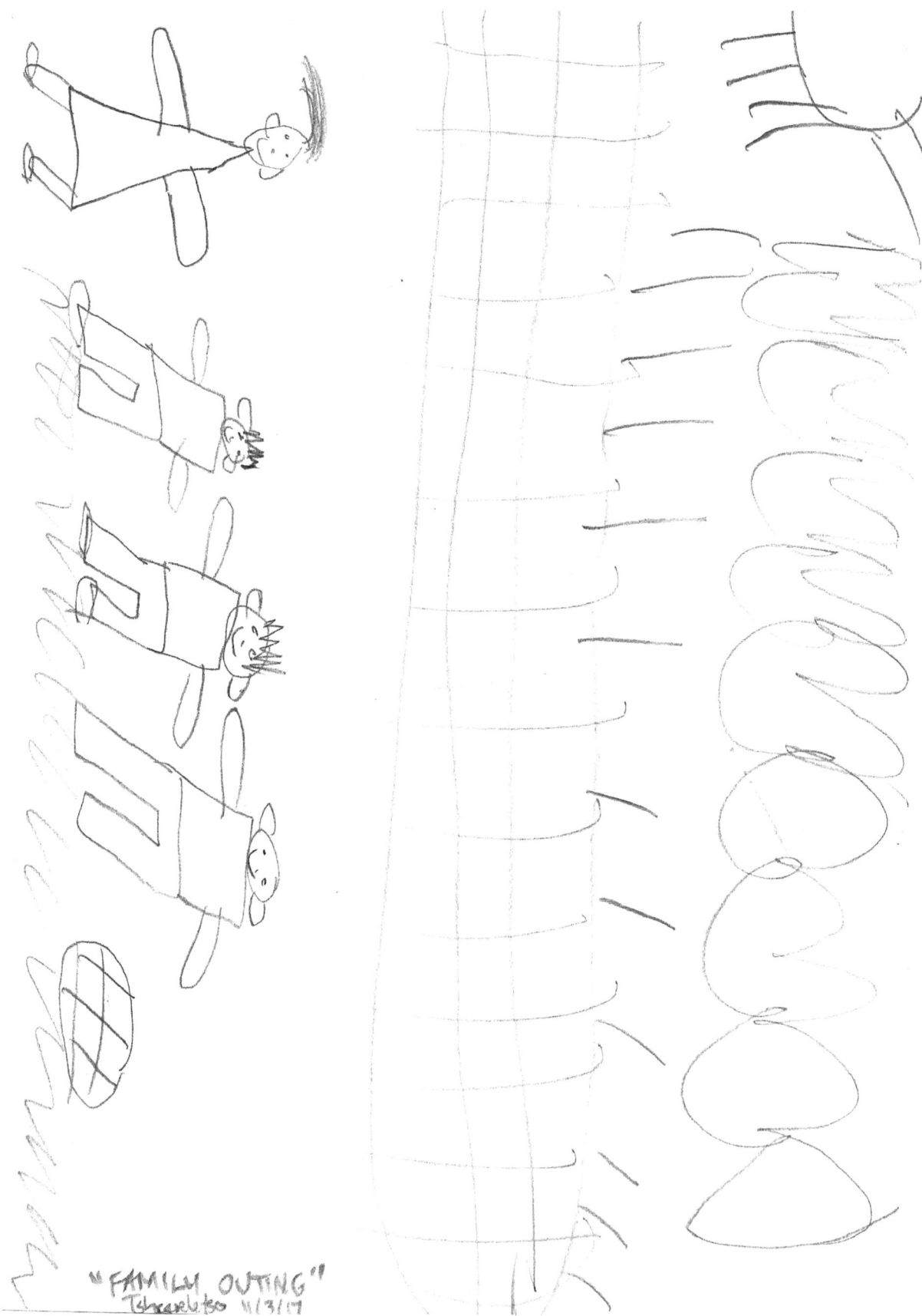

"FAMILY OUTING"
Takaru too 11/3/17

33

PULL-UP PLACE – My friends are doing pull-ups while I watch them.

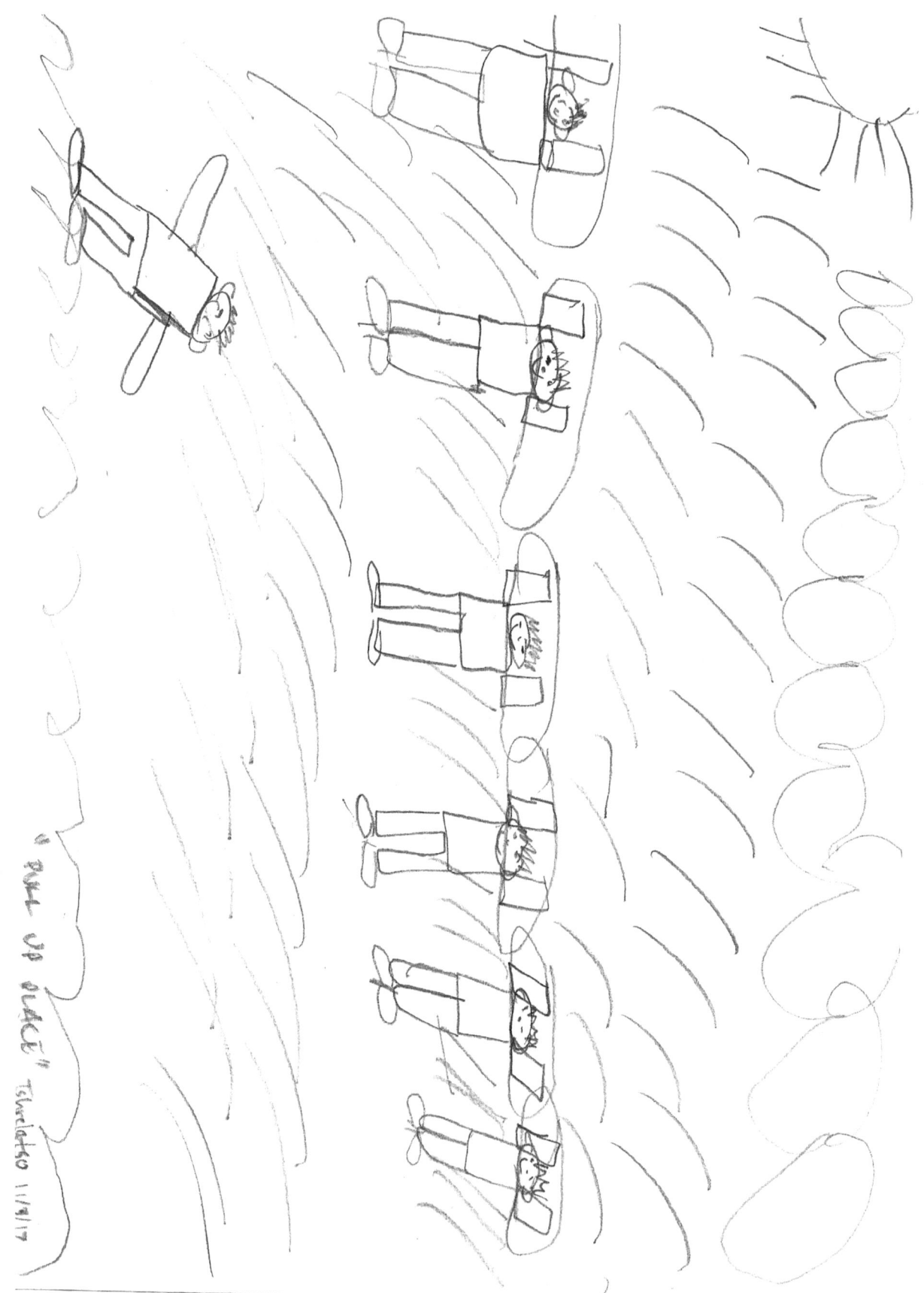

"PULL UP PLACE"
Tshiatetso 11/9/17

35

MAMLAMBO – River Queen makes the rain so that grass and trees can grow.

"MAMLAMBO" Tshcletso 11/3/17

GIVING SPACE – ME AND MY BROTHER ARE
IN OUR ROOM SO WE CAN GIVE OUR
FATHER AND MOTHER SPACE TO TALK

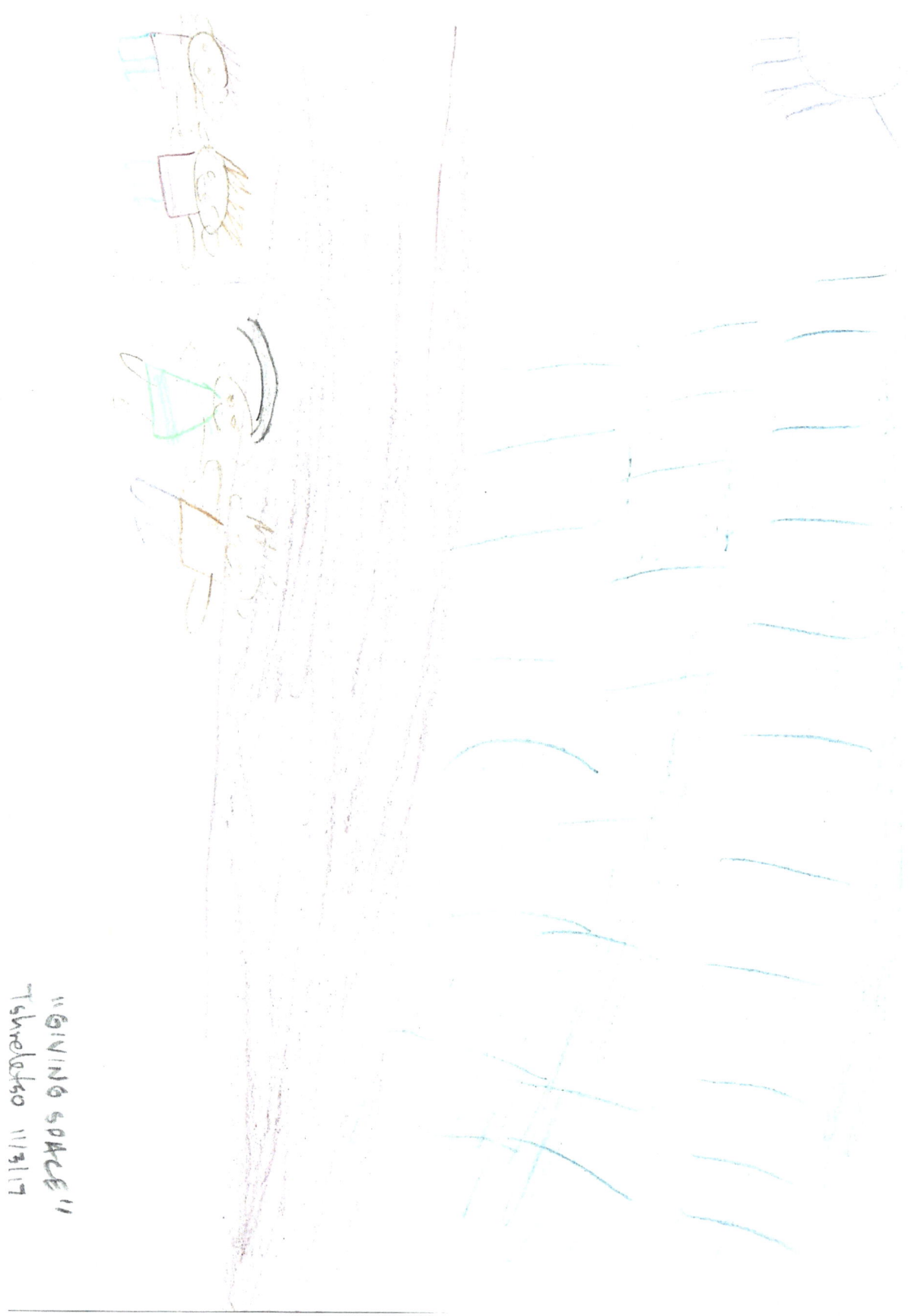

"GIVING SPACE"
Tshelatso 11/3/17

CAR STOP – The boy wants to cross 2nd Avenue, and the car stops for him.

"CAR STOP"
Tshreletso 11/9/17

SUN GAZING – ME AND MY FAMILY ARE WATCHING THE SUN.

"SUN GAZING"
Tshedatso 11/9/17

43

SOCCER MATCH – PLAYING A SOCCER MATCH WHILE PEOPLE WATCH US.

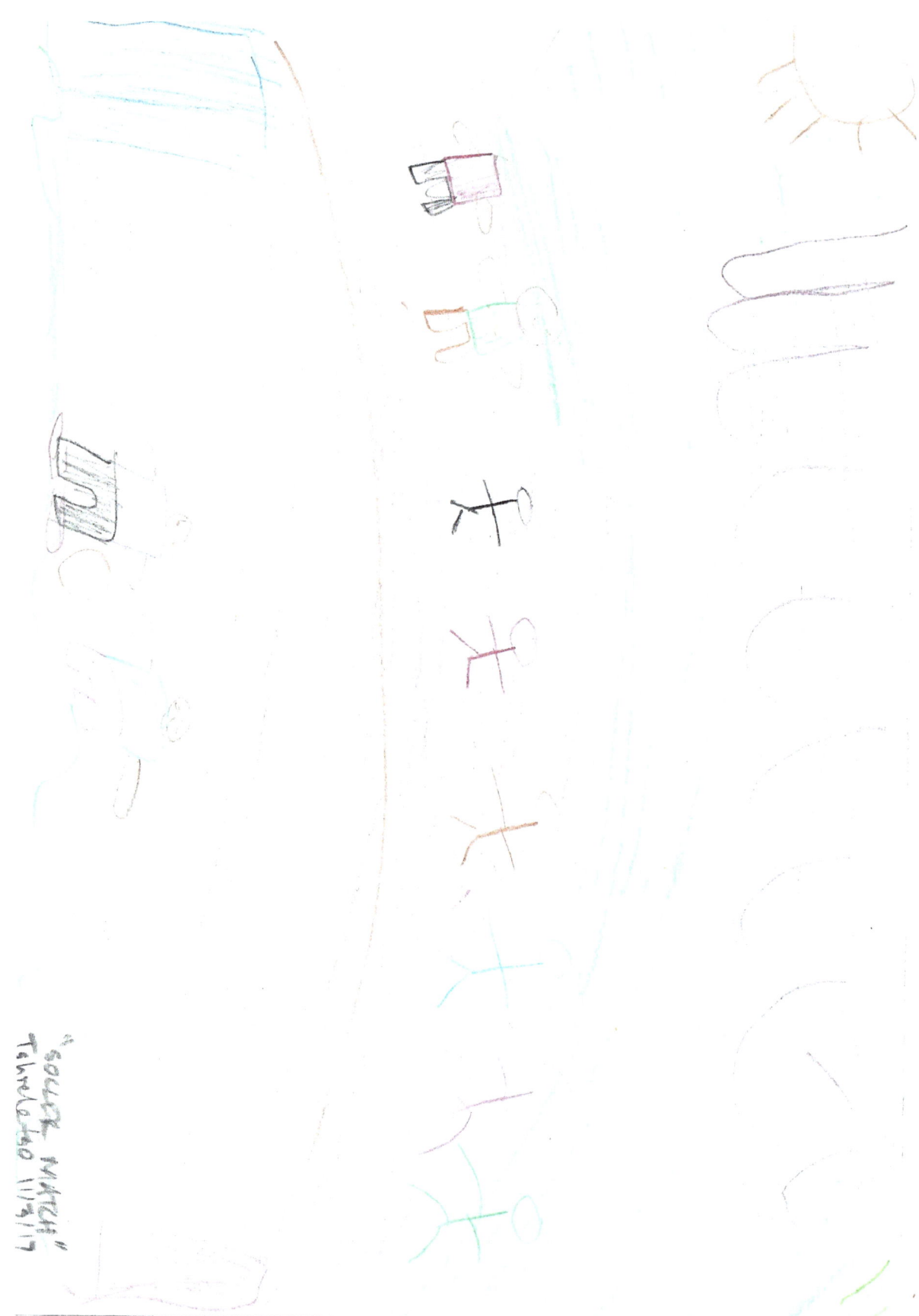

"SOCCER MATCH"
Ishmael 11/3/17

45

www.ingramcontent.com/pod-product-compliance
Lightning Source LLC
Chambersburg PA
CBHW040751200526
45159CB00025B/1842